James Manlow's poems have appeared in various magazines and journals and won prizes in competitions. He studied at the University of Derby and the University of East Anglia, and was an Arvon Jerwood Young Poet.

In December 2013 he was appointed Poet Laureate for Bournemouth (UK), the first for the town, where he lives with his wife and their daughter.

"James Manlow responds brilliantly to W. B. Yeats's admonition: he has learned his trade, his craft! These poems are remarkably well-made and they are also highly imaginative, playful, deadly serious, sexy, and deeply, deeply human. A terrific debut!"

Thomas Lux
Chair in Poetry, Georgia Institute of Technology

"The quietly understated writing in *When We Were Slugs* sidles in close to us and succeeds, through the poetry of things rather than overt ideas or emotions, in reaching unexpected depths of dislocation, dissociation and engagement. From the controlled decor of cosmonauts' apartments to a legacy rule-of-thumb for three-pin plugs, from gaming arcades to a 17c domestic genre painting, James Manlow selects eclectically to create a universe of feeling."

Anne-Marie Fyfe
Former Chair of the Poetry Society (UK)

www.parkgatepress.com

WHEN WE WERE SLUGS

www.prometheuspoetry.com

Publishers Online!

For updates and more resources, visit Prometheus Poetry and Parkgate Press online at

www.prometheuspoetry.com
www.parkgatepress.com

Page layout by Prometheus Poetry
Cover art and inside illustrations by Diana Paola Valero

ISBN-13: 978-1937056-88-9

Library of Congress Control Number: 2014952164
Library of Congress Subject Headings:

Love Poetry
Love Poetry, English
Nature--Poetry
Poetry

First Edition (worldwide) December 2014
[Parkgate Press: Prometheus Poetry reference: 018]

To Moni

Cover art and inside illustrations by
Diana Paola Valero

ACKNOWLEDGEMENTS

Acknowledgements are due to the editors and judges of the following publications and competitions, where some of these poems first appeared, won prizes or were shortlisted: *The North, Saint Ann's Review, Smith's Knoll* ; the UK National Poetry Competition, The Bridport Prize and The Arvon International Poetry Competition.

I am grateful to the Arts Council of England for a poetry grant, and to the summer seminar writing community at Sarah Lawrence College, Broxville, New York.

CONTENTS

―――――――

WHEN WE WERE SLUGS

Poems by James Manlow

Sea Poem

Even waves have doubts sometimes,
small nigglings of mistrust crawling
between their folds. Constantly trawling,
they confess their crimes
periodically upon the sand:
two hubcaps, one shoe, a tampon,
some sunglasses, a comb, a condom,
like opened letters from another land
for anyone picking about the docks
to find and interpret,
while every wave rising to its limit
breaks, wary of and wanting the rocks.
The sea can't control what's found;
only go on making that tender, restless sound.

Picture Postcard: Great Yarmouth

The buildings are postmodern-derelict,
Packaged Victorian architecture
For export to L.A.: *The Silver Slipper,*
The Showboat and *The Golden Nugget,*
Where plump, no-nonsense vendors ply their trade:
Two pounds for ice-cream; three, for pony trips;
Still less than Harry Ramsden's fish and chips,
Now found in the exquisite Merf's Arcade.

I turn, walk back the way I came, past reels
Of neon shop signs switching on: 'New:
The Amazonia Tropical Zoo!';
The stands of Norfolk mussels, jelly eels.
I stop at one to buy some prawns to eat
Then watch the sea come in. It's almost dark.
It spits with rain. Later, in the car park,
A lone youth slashes a tarpaulin sheet.

The Pencil Case

So I go with your Mum
to collect your ashes in a porcelain urn.
A week since policemen from Thames Valley
found their missing person.

At the crematorium they ask who I am.
"Neighbour," I stutter. "Friend."
'Susan' clutches my arm.
My age, you were still in uniform

when they checked for marks
behind the neck, between the toes.
Now there's been some mix up about the urn,
whether or not she wanted one.

So they hand you over in the usual plastic case,
a shiny off-grey colour, zip running along one side.
It's a pencil case. I'm certain
she must be thinking the same thing.

How will she be able to open it,
knowing that's how needles are found,
as if just another necessary instrument -
protractor, ruler, calculator?

Afterwards, I drive her home. She gets out;
I watch her shape retreat toward

the empty house where more
and more she busies herself with books,

the word *heroin* second nature
after *loving* and *daughter.*

The Brooch

I remember the storm because it broke the day you left,
raised two slabs on the swept patio,
carried the fence clean away.

Ever since, a telephone receiver
cradled in the forked branch of the sycamore,
umbilical cord severed and slow swaying.

For months I watched that pendulum,
clocking the time I had to forget you,
wondering what it was I did wrong,

that final something
muzzling your voice like a curfew.
Please, don't show up,

like this, out of the blue,
the figure from my sleep, proffering
a butterfly in your outstretched hand.

Is it to say I do not wear
my heart enough upon my sleeve,
that you pin it there, smoothing my lapel,
as if you are about to speak?

Colleagues

The after-hours stillness.
Those computers, closed down.
Laughter, unfamiliar.
Alcohol for everyone.

They will think of you
when informing your replacement
and erasing your voice
from the answer machine.

The Moon Men

Each room follows the same pattern: bygone and modern.
Gagarin's woven bedspread, an elegant compliment
to the white lace curtains in his Moscow flat;

Rauschenbakh's oak parquet floor,
the blue silk hangings and bamboo-print cushions,
a turquoise telephone on a Chinese urn;

Korolev's large windows inviting light to bleach
the flock wallpaper and standard lamp shades
dyed their mustard yellows and grass greens.

Displayed on each man's desk, a silver model rocket,
posed to take off, as if somewhere along the way
those boyish dreams, sex and space, just got mixed up.

Flight Attendance

Up here she is a film-star at first sight.
Is she so carefree really? Does she dress
This way at home - shoes off, the house a mess?
What book beside her bed last thing at night?

How often life feels like some long-haul flight.
At times of troubled turbulence, who might
Not, nearing destination, yet confess
A wish for company, a guide to bless
The journey home, towards that steady light?
A Holy One. Air angel. Soul stewardess.

Exits are here, on both the left and right.

Marilyn

In childhood where does sadness go?
Into old bottles that she fills
With daisies, grass, dead daffodils.
As though the luxury were love
She drinks glass after cold glass of
The Lady's lavender water.

This 'lady' hardly knows her daughter -
A girl at school they call 'the mouse'
Who wears because she has no blouse
A tight tan sweater (with no bra)
And skirts three sizes small and far
Too tight about her rounding hips.

Her blond highlights and lipsticked lips
Coax strangers' smiles all over town
When she goes walking up and down
Los Angeles' wide boulevards,
Far from the homes of movie-stars
Like Clarke Gable and Jean Harlow.

Towards the bright lights she brings her sorrow,
Thinking, tomorrow, tomorrow, tomorrow.

Fields

New dew, new sky, new sun,
and your face upon the makeshift pillow.
Words for our actions, you whispered one,
but not for what was lost.
Since then, our lives.

This evening on the long drive home
I can almost smell the prickling, chafing heat,
hear the name beneath the moan.
A startled deer, bare breasted,
up to her waist in wheat.

Light

I'd watch you working with a teenage son's
Lukewarm enthusiasm, loath to learn
A single thing about electric light
In desktop lamps; but you'd go on, well meaning,
Unscrewing plugs, still wanting me to understand.
"*Blue* is for *neu*tral. That's your grandfather's

Old trick," you'd say, winking like the TV fathers
When passing down such wisdom to their sons.
"Yellow and green are flowers. Understand?
They grow in *earth*... Well, stay awhile; you'll learn.
Brown *is* the colour of the earth, meaning
Where flowers live—*alive* in sunlight.

So brown is *live*." How could I know that light
Was not the point, or that my grandfather's
'Old trick' was actually a poem meaning
Love, such as only fathers bear for sons?
Then I was young and never seemed to learn
To rewire anything; distracted, I'd just stand

Watching over you. How did you ever stand
My giving in and living with a broken light?
Or not take to heart such reluctance to learn?
Your patience was unusual, a father's
Own refusal to make his ways his son's,
Even when my boredom grew demeaning.

13

Dad, it's taken over twenty years, meaning
Now, when my wife kneels down beside our nightstand
For me to show her how, it's with your son's
Full pride, I say, "*Blue*'s *neu*tral," and speak of
            sunlight,
All that stuff about flowers. "That's my father's
'Old trick,' I say. It takes a while to learn

There are no lessons that we cannot learn
With time. Time is a meaning
By which I know that one day with a father's
Quiet love before my child I too will stand
To change a cheap fuse in some ordinary light.
For now I write this poem as your son's

Own way to say how proud I am to understand
The meaning of that love's enlightenment,
When sons become their fathers; fathers, sons.

The Pyramid

Khaki is the colour of the daylight
soldiers queue and clown in, gesturing
with cigarettes—faint sweeps of smoke,
stepping in and out
of the pyramid's shadow;
my grandfather among them.

A holiday here, his half smile
lies to a woman waiting in a room
he furnishes in his mind. My grandmother
is no more than a waltz to him,
a rushed kiss fumbled in a cloakroom,
a promise whispered with hot breath.

Yet I gaze out through him. He appears
to have requisitioned my nose;
our eyebrows meet in the middle.
"Don't worry," he seems to say,
"I'm looking after these pieces of you."
But khaki is the colour of sepia;

ink fades, like my grandfather's memory,
whatever he was thinking.
My mother isn't in the desert.

Nor am I. I'm nothing,
not even a dead man.

The Dressing

The man had no skin: he was raw flesh open to the
    grit of ash and wind.
His kneecaps and elbows peeked white and brilliant;
    his forehead and chin
were bone, so that except for his cheeks, his face was
    a bright skull.
Yet he was standing, this man who had walked from
    the explosion,
as if it were a point of contest. He stood in silence, his
    throat burnt and bleeding.

I thought, *Somebody should scream for him*, but there was
    no sound,
except nurse Reynolds retching, the engines turning
    over, and far off
the dull thud of the shelling. The surgeon thrust his
    hands in his pockets.
"Morphine," he said, "as much as you want." Then he
    turned
and trampled back through the mud, his white coat
    stiff and splattered.

I walked him to the barn, promenaded through the
    camp, a lieutenant
on my arm, as though I were attending a dance.
    Inside, I made up a bed
using blankets and straw, but still he refused to lie

down, just stood there,
bleeding and quivering, out of the wind, while I
tapped a syringe
against the edge of a beam, then inserted the needle
straight into the flesh.

Nothing registered on his blank face. I wasn't even
sure he could see me.
Eventually, he tired of standing, tottered, then
collapsed to the floor.
I made him as comfortable as I could. He lay on his
back, and I could hear
the pain in his breathing—a sharp rasping, growing
steadier
as the morphine set in. When he tried to speak—a
splutter—

I leaned close. "Dress me," he said. I nodded,
unravelling a thin layer of gauze.
"No." He clutched my apron. "Dress me." Leaving
him,
I crossed the camp to the old school, where the
soldiers were laid in rows
and propped against walls. A wolf whistle rose from
one corner, where two Italians
with bright bandaged legs, were rolling cigarettes on
the back of a book.

I marched over. "I need your clothes." I got his jacket
and a vest,

but his trousers were split right up to his waist and
      tied to a splint.
The other one offered his boots. It wouldn't be a
      dress uniform
but it would do. I returned to the barn. I was too late.
      I stood
above the dead wet body, holding a pair of black
      polished boots.

Red Eye

Today we fly to where Herodotus was born.
The buses here have air-conditioning.
We stop to dip our toes in the Aegean,
then drive up the peninsula in the rain.
It's raining in Istanbul.
The rain becomes bells
ringing in the streets,
beating temples.
I dream my dream again:
houses bled; the city walls
sink into the Bosphorus.
I walk abroad and smoke.
The night air is soothing,
like the statues and stones.
Go see the pillars of the Hippodrome,
the Aya Sophia!
A man in a yellow jacket
says it's closed, whose cousin
is a travel agent, a carpet salesman.
We must have tea and talk with him;
then watch the sunset from the bridge
perforate the old city from the new
silently over the Mediterranean,
a public bud of snowfire.

Salt Cathedral

I thought of pickaxes piercing hallowed ground,
of monk-miners, sweat and blood.
But you just laughed
then took me by the hand.

Down there were you aware
of your own miracle? Enough to lure
the likes of me, eager to be awed.
The thing itself immense as any natural cave.

I close my eyes and see
your pale hands caressing
pews, font, altar, man-size crucifix;

before turning back to me
and stuffing three fingers in your mouth,
wincing, grinning: salt.

Delilah

has him kneel, lapping lightly at
the teardrop crying under her labia.
Holding him by the tendons of his hair,
relaxing her hand, she leaves him for her hunger,

only later opening her eyes
to look along the length of her own limbs,
discovering, as if by coincidence,
the man there, his head heavy,
magnificent and still
in the tender crux of her world.

The Lazy Maid

Chin snug in her palm, elbow
plugged firmly in the knobbly joint of her kneecap,
legs a little ajar beneath her skirts,
is sound asleep upon the stool,
dreaming of her mother teaching her
how to scrape parsnips;
which is how at 11.10 p.m.
the mistress of the house
discovers her, stares a while, then
as if almost sensing a stream of watchers on,
looks up, suddenly alive,
flush with wine and mischief,
gifting that wry-wild look
I love this painting for,
saying, *It's too late for this,*
and, *See what I put up with?*
How I adore this girl.
She won't change. It's 1655.
It's late. Let the dishes
alone. Let the cat eat the fish.

Ballet

In the office of the online museum,
twelve *Biston betulari*
pinned in a glass display case
with a collector's love. I recalled
from school, the big, Darwinian fuss.
With black veins crisscrossing,

like dried leaves carrying the ink-blood,
their martyred wings
were yellow, ochre, russet, blue.
"Look," said the curator,
The Ballets Russes,
captured, after all, on film."

He clicked an icon. One by one
I watched the tiny doll-like spectres
flit in silence over an open-air stage,
while the eyes of the dead
moths glistened,
with jealousy and rage.

When We Were Slugs

We spent long afternoons
in the brick's shade, speaking
about life, vague memories
of shells, how our ancestors
were Land-Snails and Sea-Snails.
It turned out we had both
shared the summer once sealed
to the underside of the water-meter,
the way we have secured ourselves
to bedroom, kitchen, living room,
as if we miss carrying
a house on our backs.

It was a small world then.
I think of those nights,
our glistening trails across the lawn,
how reaching the middle of the garden
we'd suck hard on the flesh
of the fallen fruit, then lean
into the sweetness and mate.

Matter

You say that we're mere matter,
quarks, electrons, atoms,
subject to gravity, star dust
brushed from the tips of a supernova
imploding in on itself. You say
that it's a matter of perspective:
a hundred thousand million stars,
and our galaxy just one
of a hundred thousand million others.
In three billion years, you say,
everything will cease to matter.
When Andromeda and the Milky Way
at last embrace, the black holes
at their dark hearts will feed again
and merge. The radiation wave
alone will hurl us out of orbit,
our atmosphere evaporate, the seas
boil off into space, you say.
Yet you won't talk about us.
I don't ask what's really the matter.

Saturday

Children spot it first: a green Rolls Royce.
Four teenage girls in burgundy emerge
to stretch their legs, unused to dresses and high heels,
enticing owners and tenants to their windows,
clutching steaming mugs, power-tools, babies,
on whom each girl practices her blush
before turning her hairdo toward the house.
At last the front door opens.

She takes a long time gliding whitely to the car.
Finally, it pulls away: a barge
containing one last, illusive hope,
the children trailing after it.

Entertaining the Dictator

Somehow we knew that the world had altered.
We knew there were charges and questions to be
      answered,
Though we'd done nothing. And no one said a word

In the big car, just stared as we were chauffeured
Through a crowd of faces—hungry, haggard.
We knew our world was being altered,

Wrapped up in fur, our silk stockings gartered,
While outside, mothers with silent children shivered,
And we did nothing, and no one said a word,

Not that we didn't care. Later, it was awkward,
Awful, performing for that paranoid bastard.
Changed in an instant, our world was altered,

Allowing our bodies to be mauled and fingered
While in the street the people were being butchered
And we could do nothing, couldn't even say a word;

But wondered what it would feel like to be murdered,
And desperately prayed for a brother with a sword.
Somehow we knew the whole world had been altered.
Yet we'd done nothing, and no one had said a word.

Roots

No mother anymore to fix her hair
Her father shows her how to plait a bridge
From living rubber, raising a cordage
Of tendrils, training them to walk on air

From one bank of the river to the other.
Their hands work side by side in a language
Still growing like the vines. Slowly the bridge
He loves becomes for her a mother figure:

When the rains fall it will keep her dry;
When the torrent rages it will stand its ground
Just like the ladder between Earth and Sky
That, fabled, fell somewhere in India.

He'd told such stories when her mother was around.
It had been his idea to call her India.

Siberia

On the last afternoon
we stood facing each other across the solid lake,
just as our guide instructed us.
We were there to breathe.

If you breathe in the morning
at that time of year,
in the middle of a Russian winter,
your breath will freeze in front of you,

fuse into a crystal
then drop to the ground,
raising a soft jangling
locals call the whispers of stars.

The Year Gone

The coldest January in years.
Ground squirrels died in their long sleep
While humans dreamed of ancient fears.
February snow was so deep
Hungry birds ate all the purple
Imperial caterpillars. March sheep
Lay down in unbiblical
Blizzards, like furry bars of soap.
Life felt fragile, brutal, tribal,
And Spring shrank to a futile hope
For daffodils on Saint David's Day.
In April, mothers helped bored children cope
With insect stings, waving away
Queen bees, applying *Wasp-eze*.
The bluebottles were late. And May
Was the driest since the nineties.
The sun came out in June and gave
Long flights for new butterflies
Blasted away by a wave
Of gales in July blowing westwards.
Some honey when the bees were brave.
In August, dragonflies bred in their hordes
And large numbers of Eurasian cranes
Re-colonized the Norfolk Broads.
Moods lightened. Early September rains
Brought a bumper crop of berries

And hedgerow fruit. The weathervanes
Spun on their ends, as though the Furies
Had come to turn the leaves early
With October frost. The big trees
In calm weather put on a free
Autumn colour show. November
Rainfall quenched wild grassland fungi.
The year gone seemed by December
Like a dream or a voice or a word
Humans could hardly remember.
And a bitter start to winter for the birds.

Also by Parkgate Press
(Dionysus Books)

www.parkgatepress.com
www.dionysusbooks.com

Josh Green
DIRTYVILLE RHAPSODIES

Do you really know your neighbors, America?

This short story collection focuses on ordinary people caught in all manner of conundrums and fiascos, much of it their own stinking fault. Some of them will weave meaning from disaster and stupidity. And some won't.

Tom Robertson

NAPOLEON Vs. THE TURK

When the Master Warrior Met the Master Machine

A play based on the chess match of Napoleon Bonaparte and 'The Turk,' the famous 18th century chess automaton. Who will triumph, the master tactician or the technology? First performed at the Toronto Fringe Festival.

www.ingramcontent.com/pod-product-compliance
Lightning Source LLC
Chambersburg PA
CBHW021147020426
42331CB00005B/940